The Caterpillar & the Spider

Lux Luther

Cadmus Publishing
www.cadmuspublishing.com

Copyright © 2022 Lux Luther

Published by Cadmus Publishing
www.cadmuspublishing.com
Port Angeles, WA

ISBN: 978-1-63751-243-2

All rights reserved. Copyright under Berne Copyright Convention, Universal Copyright Convention, and Pan-American Copyright Convention. No part of this book may be reproduced, stored in a retrieval system, or transmitted in any form, or by any means, electronic, mechanical, photocopying, recording or otherwise, without prior permission of the author.

This is a work of fiction; therefore, names, characters, places, and incidents are the products of the author's imagination or are used fictitiously. Any resemblance to actual events, locales, or persons, living or dead, is entirely coincidental.

Table of Contents

Afterlife 1
The Homecoming 4
From Flight to Fright 10
Former Tadpole & Former Flyer Collide 15
Color Uncoordinated 21
A Preying Mantic Butterfly 28
Seventh Retrospection 38
The Wisdom Lying Somewhere Between the Butterpillar & the
    Caterfly 55

First Retrospection

Afterlife

As he crawled along the ground slowly, and gracefully, he paused for short periods of time to observe other life forms he was surrounded by.

He realized that in comparison to so many of the other creatures, he was very limited in his ability to make it to many of the same locations. Being trapped in spots, or stuck on his back, unable to regain his footing for hours at a time, seemed like many lifetimes in duration to this little creature.

However, he felt a strong propellant force within himself telling him that someday he would rise above his circumstances, and become envied by the others who were presently in a more favorable position than he.

He always noticed that a creature in a silky-looking artifice, in the corner of a nearby house, with eight legs, was very practical, and clever, and paying special attention to him. He watched this crafty individual trap, and devour a countless number of unsuspecting victims, and knew he never wanted to be another one of them.

Meanwhile, this eight-legged wonder was trying to figure out how it could get the crawling, beautiful multi-colored Earth worm into its web. It was going to be much harder since it never left the ground, or would ever accidentally fly into its invisible web like so many of its other meals.

Until one day he was surprised by being unable to find the multi-colored beautiful crawler anymore. However, he did notice a strange, thick, and silky-looking contraption developing on the lower side of the same house his web was attached to.

He tried to break in, but found it to be like a little jail cell protecting a prisoner on the inside he was forbidden to get at, or even see. He watched this strange-looking ornament pass through a series of transformations, which confirmed the suspicions he held about something being inside of it. But what was it?

It became really ugly, and pitch black in color. So he thought maybe it was dying, or dead, and would soon disappear. Soon afterwards though, some colorful tips protruded from the black oviform shell, that made him extremely apprehensive. So he decided to allow this process to continue uninterruptedly to see what the final outcome would bring. A few days later he glanced at the spot again, only to find that the oviform structure was gone. The only sign of it was a few black shreds lying on the ground beneath where it once hung.

After a short period of time elapsed, and the eight-legged predator had almost forgotten about what he'd been studying, a beautiful winged creature was sitting on the edge of the roof of the house, staring down at him reposed in his web.

The hunter suddenly realized it possessed the same colors as the funny shapes emerging from the black vehicle a few days before. So when the winged creature was certain its nemesis was watching, he gracefully flew from the edge of the house, shot a proud glance at the killer as it flew by, winked, and then disappeared.

The predatory killer sat in its web for a while, and reflected long and hard. He realized that the marvelous multi-colored Earth worm was the same color as the beautiful flying creature who gave him that unforgettable proud glance.

He thought back to the time when he had been in a more superior position than the pretty Earth worm, who had now become the object of his envy, because he knew he would always remain a web spinning eight-legged predator.

Second Retrospection

The Homecoming

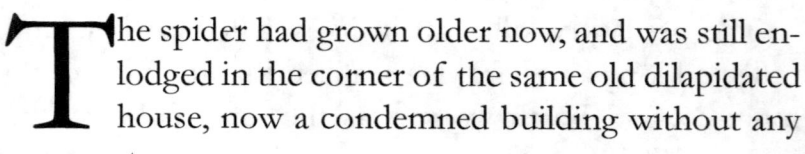

The spider had grown older now, and was still enlodged in the corner of the same old dilapidated house, now a condemned building without any occupants.

Word had been getting back to him for years about the philanthropic reputation of the old caterpillar he'd seen morph into the most lovely butterfly, and all of the joy and wonder he'd been evoking in the hearts of so many people up and down the East Coast.

The spider had been brooding, and plotting ever since the day the butterfly gave him that glance, over how he was going to turn him back into the mere wriggling worm he originally was.

He realized he did not possess the mobility, power, or skill required to pull it off alone, but felt he knew the perfect someone to help if he could convince him of how worthless the butterfly had been before, so he decided to go visit the neighborhood bull frog, and discuss his malicious intentions.

When he finally found him he asked if he remembered the caterpillar who was now the butterfly, and coastal legend. The frog said he remembered him well, and hated him too, because he was able to transform himself into someone much greater than he was capable of ever doing. He told the spider that the butterfly reminded him of the days when he was just a little tadpole in a large pond. That his transformation into a land creature who is able to roam the land, or return to the water if necessary, but never fly, caused him to envy the butterfly for having the freedom to fly wherever his little heart desired.

He also felt that everyone along the coast should be made aware of the butterfly's past, and how it used to be an insignificant little caterpillar. He told the spider he would love to assist him in bringing about the well-deserved downfall of the caterpillar.

They preferred referring to him as "that caterpillar", because that's how they wanted to always remember him. It helped them forget about their own inferiority complexes long enough to feel better within themselves about what they were planning to do.

The frog expressed to the spider how he was just as him, and did not have it within himself what it took to bring the butterfly down either, but that he knew a friend who could probably help them. His friend was a chameleon, and so they went where the frog knew they'd probably spot him.

They found him on the trunk of a dark brown tree. The chameleon blended in perfectly with the tree bark to camouflage himself from the snakes and rodents that were lurking around during this time of the day.

The spider was very impressed by the skill of the chameleon, and how it would be a very useful tool for strategically entrapping the butterfly. They got straight to the point, and were delighted to find out they had another ally who would assist them in bringing him down. He told them he would love to use his gift from nature to punish someone he too envied with a passion, and would use his color changing to set the perfect trap. He was sure he could make the butterfly his friend by discussing the colors they had in common, and commending the butterfly's superiority over him of being permanently multi-colored.

He believed a little ego stroking was definitely in order here, and highlighted how he never failed to adapt to every personality he had ever encountered. The chameleon said his friend, the praying mantis, could outthink the butterfly, and could fly much faster. That the butterfly would be no match for the praying mantis because he was humble enough to attract the butterfly, making it the perfect distraction for concealing his killer instinct. He hoped the praying mantis would be willing to use its skills to put the butterfly back in its place when the opportunity presented itself.

So when the butterfly flew back into his old neighborhood for a visit, he went straight to the old house where he underwent his most memorable metamorphosis, and immediately caught a glimpse of the same old spider web in the same corner of the house.

He flew by to see if his old stalker friend was home, and of course he was, since he'd been patiently awaiting the butterfly's return. The spider told him the news of his success had reached him, and how proud he was of the fact that an old acquaintance was able to leave the neighborhood and become so well known, and admired by everyone the way he had. He also shared that he had a couple of new friends who knew about him as well, and how anxious they were to meet him.

So they met up with the frog first, and the butterfly took the initiative to tell the frog the reasons why he should be delighted to know the two of them were both morphogenic creatures unique in their own ways. He said that nature just intended for him to fly, and be much more naturally talented, and beautiful than him, and so many others, but would love it if the two of them could remain friends.

The frog smiled, while hiding the fact of how incensed he was by the condescending remarks the butterfly made, and told him he had a chameleon friend who was also anxious to make his acquaintance. So they made their way to the chameleon thereafter who happened to be sunbathing on a huge rock when they found him.

The butterfly introduced himself while resting on the friendly frog's back. While they got to know each other a little better the spider, frog, and chameleon indulged one another in friendly conversation, mainly about the butterfly's exciting adventures, and all the people's lives he touched. Then he shared with them how deeply he regretted not being able to bring all of them along on his up and coming ventures, but that he promised to keep them always in his heart.

That's when the spider and the frog decided it was time to say their goodbyes. The moment of the butterfly's impending doom was vastly approaching, and they needed to get into their positions.

So while the chameleon and the butterfly got better acquainted the chameleon used every opening in the conversation as an opportunity for sliding in his deceptive flattery. Just as planned, he stroked the butterfly's ego about its hypnotic colors, and skillfulness in flying, until his defenses were all the way down.

The sun was fading fast. The butterfly lost track of the chameleon, and the spider and frog hid in the bushes nearby waiting to see what the clever chameleon had planned for their fairweather friend.

Then the Almighty praying mantis flew right up next to the butterfly and said, "Hello. I've been sent on a mission to you by our friend the chameleon, and if you don't mind my saying so, but you are even more beautiful than he described. He also informed me that you would love a companion to go along with you on your next adventure, and I was hoping to have the fortune of being that chosen one, because I, like you, can fly too."

The butterfly blushed and said, "I think that would be a wonderful idea. Are you ready to get started?"

The praying mantis said, "Let us pray first," and then they took to the sky.

While in midair the praying mantis took his powerful praying hands, and clipped the majestic wings of the butterfly, and then said as he fell right in between the laughing spider, frog, and chameleon, "May God bless you, you beautiful, foolish caterpillar!"

Third Retrospection

From Flight to Fright

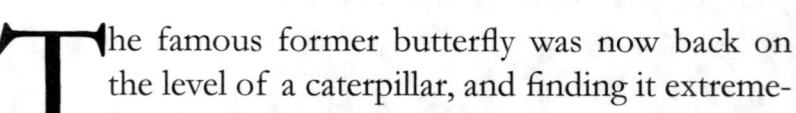

The famous former butterfly was now back on the level of a caterpillar, and finding it extremely difficult to acclimate, and adapt to the sudden changes he was being forced to endure.

Having been reduced to crawling around on the ground again, and loss of that exaggerated sense of self-importance he'd gotten too comfortable with, due to the philanthropic reputation he established along the coast. He had nubs in the place where his wings once were. He wondered if there was some remote possibility for being blessed to regrow a full set of wings as beautiful as the ones he lost, but had somewhat of a pessimistic outlook, knowing that such a thing had never occurred in Nature before.

He eventually made his way back to his old stomping grounds. He reminisced about how hard life had been before he underwent the metamorphosis which helped to make life so much easier. How having the freedom to just pick up and move, or go wherever his heart desired were the happiest times of his life.

The idea of never being able to experience such unbounded joy and freedom again finally brought him to tears.

While he was crying he heard a familiar sound above his head, and looked up to find his old spider friend hanging by a thread. He just hung there staring with a confused look, yet very far from empathetic.

"Why do you cry, my friend? Why do you cry, my old fallen star of a friend?" he said.

"Just look at me!" said the former flyer. "Just look at me! I never imagined I would ever be in this miserable position again. Crawling around on the ground for food, being stuck in places, and on my back for over extended periods of time, having to always look over my shoulder, or above my head for fear of being overpowered, ambushed, or trampled upon.

"I'm meaningless down here, in contrast to who I was before that pseudo praying mantis clipped my wings. I just don't know if I can ever readjust to living this way again?"

"Well my fallen star of a friend, do you have any idea why the praying mantis would do such a thing to someone as noble, and perfect as yourself? I mean, the two of you had just met for the first time, right? I don't see any reason why someone you have never done anything to would want to ruin your life like this. Can you?"

"That's a good question. I've been groveling around down here trying to figure out how someone I just met would suddenly desire to cripple me like this. I'm as harmless and gentle as anyone could ever expect anyone to be. Mr. Spider, can you think of any reason why anyone would wish to humiliate me?"

The spider then lowered himself on the thread he was dangling from and said, "I'm not sure my fallen friend, but I'm convinced that if you take a hard, honest look within you will find the answers you are so desperately seeking. I mean, you've been up and down the East Coast, and mingled with a diverse amount of personalities in your quest for greatness. So you must've learned some very valuable lessons about yourself, and the affect you have on others not so gifted as yourself?"

As he began slowing easing his way back up the thread he hung from, all of a sudden the Earth started quaking violently. The former flyer quickly scoped out a nearby hole he immediately sought safety in. On his way to it he looked to determine whether or not the spider made it back into the corner of the house yet, only to notice the horrifying sight of the house crumbling to the ground.

He yelled at the top of his little lungs from the hole, hoping to summon the spider to join him, but the dust, flying objects, and quaking of the Earth made it too difficult to focus on any particular thing.

Once the storm subsided the former flyer emerged from the hole searching for the spider, and heard him calling for his help. Since the former flyer no longer had its wings he couldn't reach his old friend as quick and easy as he wished. He crawled as fast as he could with tears of pain and frustration falling, from feelings of helplessness, hopelessness, and powerlessness he believed he would've never been held captive by again.

By the time he reached his friend, who lie nearly crushed to death underneath pieces of wood from the fallen house, he was breathing his last breaths.

As the spider died he looked into the eyes of his former flying friend and said, "Don't cry, or have pity on me, my old buddy. You must not feel sorry for me because what is happening to me right now is happening to you also, and is part of life. I have served my purpose as a spider in this life, and the last part of it is to tell you this. I watched you transform from a crawling caterpillar into a beautiful butterfly who became the envy of nearly everyone in this region you left behind, and that was a very great accomplishment for you. You probably believed it was a very inspirational occurrence for anyone who witnessed your change, but the one memory that shines the brightest in my mind more vividly than anything about you my old foolish friend, is that day I looked and saw you perched on the edge of the roof with those beautiful new set of wings; and the way you shot me that soul piercing, arrogant, proud, condescending, and vain glorious wink, and then flew away.

"That is my most lasting memory of you, and it's the very reason why you're crawling on the ground again. Since Nature's clock prohibits me from getting into greater detail, I suggest you devote some time and energy into finding our old friend the bull frog.

"Tell him about my passing, and would the two of you please protect the eggs I laid recently. Make sure you ask him why the praying mantis clipped your wings. He will have more information for you my foolish former flying friend," and then he was gone.

Fourth Retrospection

Former Tadpole & Former Flyer Collide

"I got here as fast as I could! What happened? I was floating in the pond on a log when everything started shaking. So, I just hopped into the water to be safe, but I did see the old house falling before I made it underwater. Are you alright though?"

"Yes, I'm fine," said the former flyer, "but I can't say the same for our old friend here. He was on his way back to his web when the Earth started quaking. He was caught by surprise, and unable to make it to safety before the decrepit house gave in, and collapsed on him. I hid in that little hole right over there. See it?

"His last words to me were that I should find you, because you would have some answers for me about why the praying mantis decided to render me wingless;

and for you and I to oversee its unhatched eggs and make sure nothing tampers with them. He said you knew where they should be."

The old bull frog just squatted there motionless, and grieved over the loss of his old friend. The gruesome sight of his little crushed frame was to him a sure sign, and a reminder that everyone shall surely reap everything they've sown.

Pains of sharp guilt crept up on him as well over the fact that his former flying friend could have died too without the assistance of the beautiful wings he'd played a significant role in him losing. It was in this very moment he began looking at life through a different lens, and a paralyzing fear of what lie around the corner suddenly overtook him.

He wondered if whether or not what happened to the spider was directly connected to what they'd all recently done to the former flyer. So he used some of his quiet time to figure out exactly what to tell him about why the praying mantis clipped his wings.

Suddenly the former flyer began shaking violently, convulsing. Then the bull frog saw one of the most bizarre, and miraculous things it had ever seen. He saw the nubs where the former flyer's wings once were; he saw them begin to slowly grow back towards the sky. He just sat there and watched in amazement, trying to interpret the message he knew Nature must've been sending him. An explanation for the bizarre series of events he'd witnessed in such a short span of time.

"Ah! Ah! What happened? What just happened?" said the former flyer, as he came back to his senses.

"That's what I'm trying to figure out. All of a sudden you started freakin' out, and totally scared the wits out of me, but I do have a startling revelation for you. You may not believe this, but your wings are coming back. I sat here and watched them grow with my own two eyes, and I probably wouldn't have believed it had I not seen it myself, but it's true, they're coming back. Have you taken a look at yourself since you lost your wings?"

"Well I stopped at the pond earlier and saw a reflection of myself in the water, and my wings were pretty much all gone. Anyway, why do you ask?"

"Because I wanna take you back to the pond, and show you the proof of what I just told you. So get on my back, and let's go!"

After getting over his apprehensiveness from memories of what happened the last time he was on the bull frog's back, he slowly inched his way up there, and they made their way to the pond. When they reached it the bull frog said, "Okay my friend, look. Look at your reflection in the water."

It was true, just as the bull frog had said. The former flyer's nubs were now stubby wings. The former flyer couldn't believe what he was seeing, but had no other choice than to submit to what the water reflected back at him…

He tried to feel the new growth, but was unable to. So it became apparent to him at that moment he was going to have to patiently persevere in spite of his turbulent emotional condition.

Even though the former flyer had lost its wings, it still had the body of a butterfly, but with less fluidity than it had as a caterpillar. So its new way of living was for the former flyer, synonymous with death. When it was able to witness for itself the new growth of its wings it said, "Until now I thought I was surely going to die, and ready to just give up altogether. If it had not been for the love and support of you and our late, beloved friendly spider, I may have passed on even before the Earthquake hit, but now I'm beginning to feel a deep sense of hope. So tell me old, great bull frog, why did the praying mantis do this awful injustice to little, innocent, old me. Why?"

The bull frog said, "I'm not 100% sure, but I'd like to share with you what I experienced while I was underwater during the Earthquake. I saw a significant amount of tadpoles while I waited for the cataclysm to subside. They reminded me of my younger years in the pond as a tadpole, feeling helpless, and scared nearly all the time. Always hoping that someday I'd become something better and more capable.

"When I started developing my arms and legs, and my body began evolving I was extremely elated, and looked forward to a life on land someday; which leads me to the main reason why I am sharing my eye opening experience with you now.

"It was only during this most life-threatening moment that I've been able to get a more holistic perspective on life, and all other living things. I started reflecting upon the role other creatures besides myself play in the economy of Nature, and how some things are intended to remain just as they are for a time, while some evolve, but that everything in Nature is moving towards a higher state of consciousness. It seems as though everything high must be brought low, only to rebecome greater through its own efforts, and by learning the lessons necessary for raising its awareness during the journey.

"I guess what I'm really trying to say to you my former flying friend is that, some of us out here in the wild never come to this realization about life, and ourselves. So we never learn to humbly accept our place in the ecosystem we're part of. We become obsessed with the idea of being better than, instead of better with. The spirit of competition consumes our entire being, causing us to destroy ourselves, and the system we are an extension of. We never become aware of the fact that when we hurt, or injure others in our community, that we are ultimately injuring ourselves, and too many of us pass on without ever knowing these simple truths.

"I'm truly sorry about what happened to you my former flying friend, and I sympathize with your present unfortunate condition. As for what reason the praying mantis clipped your beautiful wings, I suggest you examine your own personal transformation, and determine whether or not you've been flying too high. Nature has a unique way of utilizing its own creatures as tools for teaching its other creatures their most necessary, and valuable lessons.

"As for our old friend the spider, and its eggs, they are under the stairwell of this fallen house. Come, let me show you where they are…"

Just as they were on their way to the spot, with the bull frog leading the way, the former flyer looked to its right, and saw the neighborhood snake lunging towards the bull frog with its mouth wide open. Then it slid under a piece of wood from the fallen house, and watched as the snake slowly devoured the bull frog. As the bull frog disappeared from sight he said to the former flyer, "Go and find the chameleon my soon to be flying friend. He will explain to you what I could not, and don't forget to do what the spider asked us to do," but being careful not to tip the snake off to the fact that there were spider eggs in the vicinity.

After the snake swallowed the frog it slithered off. The former flyer sat in the same spot for a while and reflected on the day's events. He was beginning to get an idea as to why he'd been slighted in such a way, and was ready to learn more now. He also starting to feel the small growth of his wings which were now almost halfway back. He was anxious, and hopeful, but knew he had to find the chameleon, and set out to do just that.

Fifth Retrospection

Color Uncoordinated

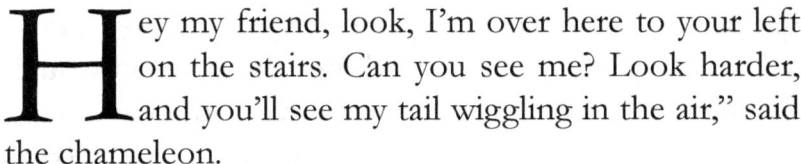

"Hey my friend, look, I'm over here to your left on the stairs. Can you see me? Look harder, and you'll see my tail wiggling in the air," said the chameleon.

"There's no need to go searching for me because I'm right here. In fact I've been close by you the entire journey, but you just never saw me, because you just couldn't see me. I hid myself in a hole not far from the one you squirmed your way into as the storm began that killed our friendly neighborhood spider. I've been watching everything from different locations, but I never allowed for myself to be detected. I was waiting to see if you would become more self-aware of how your behavior is, and it's been affecting others in your environment.

So, tell me my former flying friend, what have you to say for yourself."

"Well first of all I'd like to know why you disappeared that evening just before the Almighty praying-mantis clipped my wings. Where did you go? And why didn't you tell me you were leaving? I mean we had just met, and I thought we were becoming friends?"

"Oh, that's what you thought my former flying friend? That we were becoming friends? Who gave you that impression? I had no idea we were becoming friends. I've never had a single friend in my life, but only other creatures around me who by observing, and examining their behavior, have assisted me in learning more about myself, and how to adapt to our ever-changing environment.

"I've learned I'm affected by our environment regardless of what we will, and my camouflage is just the ability to adapt, and change along with it. It is through our never allowing any external environmental changes to alter our inner state of being, and then making the adjustments.

"My ability to change colors, and adapt to the multiplicity of shades I'm exposed to, is Nature's greatest gift to me. I've watched you grow from a crawling critter into one that flew, and the laws of Nature dictated that you had no other choice but to become a flyer.

"You never asked to become a butterfly, you just became one, and you did it unconsciously, and through no will or desire of your own. So my question for you is, what have you learned about yourself since you began flying, and left the environment you were raised in, only to become an East Coast legend?"

"Well, you haven't exactly explained to me your sudden disappearance on that dreadful evening, or the reasons why you left without saying anything. So before I answer any of your questions, I would really appreciate it if you answered mine!"

"Okay my former flying friend, I'll answer your questions, but if I remember correctly, your wings were completely clipped, but seem to be returning. I mean, your wings are actually coming back! Aren't they?"

The former flyer just smiled.

"But anyway," said the chameleon, "to answer your first question my former flyer, I will say that I didn't disappear. What actually occurred was that the Earth rotated away from the light of the Sun, causing my body to take on a shade that was impossible for you to perceive. So, to you it appeared as though I was gone. I was actually with you up until the time when you and the praying mantis said that long pre-flight prayer. I left while the two of you were praying to join the spider and the frog.

"I waited around while you discussed your flight plans to see if you would recognize me, but of course you did not. Just as I predicted. Ever since I've been observing you I've noticed you don't pay attention to details, but I hoped you were going to behave differently in that instance."

"Do you have any idea why the praying mantis did such an awful thing to me? I can vividly remember him saying to be me just before we took to the sky that I was more beautiful than you had described. So it's obvious the two of you knew each other, and had had a conversation about me beforehand. Did he tell you he was planning to humiliate me? Did he express any sort of dislike for me during your talks with him?

"Please! If you know why he did this just tell me. I really need to understand what brought this unfortunate calamity upon me, and why you, the frog, and the spider were all laughing when I fell from the sky? Can you tell me what happened?"

"Well my former flying friend, let me take you back to the beginning. Like I said before I was around to witness your transformation from a caterpillar to a butterfly, and you were much more humble, empathetic, and acutely aware when you were a crawling caterpillar. Because you were so limited as a crawler, you were naturally forced to be more consciously attuned to what was around you, and your own behavior as well.

"I also saw our deceased friendly neighborhood spider, and watched him watch you. I've seen the morphological miracle of many caterpillars in my days. So, I knew you would someday be flying high like all the other caterpillars I've seen, and I waited to see if you would remember what it was like before you were able to fly.

"You see, I'm one of the most gifted, and versatile members of our little ecosystem, but your being able to fly is a gift that only you of all the land rovers possesses.

"When you left the neighborhood, and word came back to us that everyone along the East Coast was witnessing the joy of your beauty and talents, but we were the ones who watched you transform, we felt betrayed when you never even so much as sent us a message back.

"I mean, just think about it my former flying friend. Either I, the frog, and maybe even the spider could've captured, and eaten you long before you ever became a butterfly.

"However, we all felt we saw something different in you, so we decided to allow you to live, and you repaid us by leaving our ecosystem the first chance you got, and became famous."

"I thought you said before that you've never had any friends in your life. I mean, it sounds to me like you had friendship expectations of me, or like you feel as though I owe you something. Is that true?"

"Well not exactly my former flying friend. It's just that back then I was so much younger, and I sort of felt that way. As I got older I began understanding what it is to be a cooperative member of an ecosystem, and my responsibility as a co-worker with Nature.

"I learned that co-existing with others in my environment didn't necessarily have to be about friendship, but cooperation. In fact, I learned my greatest lessons about life, and myself through watching you before you left, and since you've returned. You don't owe me or anyone else a thing, but I hope you learn the lessons life is attempting to teach you through me, and our two deceased friends. If you know what I mean?"

It was now midday, and the sun was at its zenith. The former flyer turned his head for the blink of an eye, but when he turned back around he didn't see the chameleon. He started panicking, but remembered to stay calm this time, and focus harder than ever before. When he looked again, he saw the chameleon on one of the branches in a nearby tree.

"Oh there you are" said the former flyer.

"I see you now! What are you doing way up there? Don't you want to finish our conversation?"

The chameleon said, "If you would like to continue then you must come up here. It's time for you to get off the ground now anyway. Just close your mouth and concentrate on coming to me!"

So he closed his eyes and concentrated harder than he thought was possible, and all of a sudden felt that powerful, self-propelling force once again. To his great surprise he found himself in the air. He was flying with a skill and confidence far surpassing any of his previous flights. It was almost as if he'd never been without his wings at all. So he flew up to where the chameleon was, and landed on its back.

He said, "Oh my dear friend, I can't believe that this is happening to me all over again, and now the day has finally arrived. I thank you from the very depths of my spirit for all of your insightful words, and wise counsel.

Now I plan to be visiting you as often as possible in the very near future."

"Well my flying friend, I must be going now, but I'm very proud and happy for you. I hope that life will be good to you from here on out, and-."

Suddenly a massive hawk swooped down from out of nowhere, snatched the chameleon, then flew away. It frightened the butterfly a bit, but then he just sat for a while on the same tree branch, and awaited the arrival of the Almighty Praying Mantis, but this time he was ready for whatever he might have in store.

Sixth Retrospection

A Preying Mantic Butterfly

Now that his wings were back, he was trying to decide exactly how he was going to behave during his next encounter with the praying mantis. There was no denying the fact that he was still furious, and resentful over what the praying mantis did to him, but now he had to insure himself against the possibility of such a calamity ever occurring again.

Upon deeper self-reflection, the renewed butterfly realized that everything he suffered at the hands of his so-called, well-intentioned admirers, was not as awful as he once perceived them to be. In fact, he began viewing his past in a way he never imagined.

In some strange way, he viewed everything as a Divine Intervention, which made it possible for him to become a more self-aware, and highly conscious individual, who was now better equipped at seeing how his unconscious behaviors and mannerisms offended others.

The more he thought about his next encounter with the cold, calculated, and merciless praying mantis, he questioned himself as to whether or not his previous inclination for vengeance was actually self-promoting, or habitually self-defeating.

If it's true that everything which brought about his first fall from the Heavens was truly a divine intervention, then the praying mantis had only played the prescribed role Mother Nature had intended.

He decided maybe it would be better to give the praying mantis an opportunity to explain itself before taking an irretrievable action.

He remained perched on a branch amidst colorful leaves, camouflaging himself, and making it nearly impossible to be detected. He made sure to remain motionless, and keep his wings from flapping up and down nervously.

He wanted the praying mantis to be completely unaware of his presence when he finally came back through.

He planned to surprise him in the same fashion he'd been taken by surprise on that fateful evening.

He sat there motionless, breathing calmly in the same spot for two whole days waiting, but he didn't show up. However, his mind was made up that he would not be leaving a well-camouflaged location until he, and the Almighty Mantis had it out once and for all.

Then, when he'd almost completely given up hope, he saw him. Yeah, it was certainly him. He was poised on a tree not far from the one he sat, not moving either, and blending in perfectly with the surroundings.

The butterfly thought maybe he'd been overlooking him the whole time. The possibility the mantis had been there watching him for three days was horrifying, and wondered if whether or not he should just use his powerful, overwhelming energy surge to charge into the praying mantis while his back was turned, and crush its body up against the hard tree it was resting on.

Instead, he restrained himself, and decided that this time he would convert his energy, and use it effectively to take flight with his new set of wings. He was going to be mature, and rise above the underdeveloped caterpillar who still lived within him, and could surely rebecome if he ever forgot all he had been through.

As the praying mantis remained still, and motionless, the butterfly used the time to collect, and maintain his calm, and the serenity required for approaching this sleeping dragon. Ironically though, this creature he revered so much began holding a deeper significance for him. He no longer saw him as the enemy, but the necessary force of opposition who was making it possible for him to fly higher, and better than he ever had before. The resistance needed for building a set of wings capable of propelling him to unimaginable heights.

The butterfly needed to prove to himself he was capable of communicating effectively enough to overcome any resistance he might face in the future during his interactions with others who were far less confident of themselves than him. He knew the praying mantis was the perfect individual for him to test his skills on, and wasn't going to miss this once in a lifetime opportunity.

He was somewhat apprehensive about how he should approach the mantis, but then decided to just take a leap, and fly right up beside him in the most unthreatening manner possible.

So, he just flew up close to him, and hovered in the air so that the mantis had a chance to become aware of his presence. When he saw the mantis was unmoved, he landed gently beside him, and gathered himself.

Then said, "Hello, Mr. Mantis. I've been sitting close by for the past couple of days looking for you to come through, but then spotted you here just a short while ago. Do you remember me by any chance?"

"Of course I remember you, you beautiful foolish caterpillar! I mean you must really be a fool if you're approaching the very same creature who clipped your wings the first time, or if you believed for a millisecond that I didn't know you've been sitting on that tree over there for the past two and a half days. I've been waiting for you to decide what course of action you were going to take, because I'm fully equipped to deal with you according to whatever method you choose.

"If you've decided to be aggressive then I must inform you beforehand I've been forbidden to clip your wings again, but I will restrain you long enough to perform the task I've been commissioned to carry out if you force the issue.

"If you choose to take the passive approach then I don't know why you've even come here in the first place. I mean, I don't have anything to prove to you, and I'm definitely not going to apologize for what I did! I was only doing my job. If by any chance you've chosen to take my act of mercy personal then you are, and shall always remain a mere caterpillar even though you've re-grown the most beautiful set of wings."

The butterfly sat quietly, and listened carefully to the words of the mantis. They were quite disturbing at first, but then he quickly recalled all of the reasons why he had come to meet with the mantic-mantis; and it helped him respond in a sagely manner.

He said, "I didn't decide to meet with you for the sake of physical combat, or to express in some sort of passive aggressive like way, how much I resent what you did. Actually I've come here to thank you for helping me obtain the second sight I have from being brought low after having flown so high.

"When you first clipped my wings all I felt was pain and contempt. It hurt me tremendously to have to re-adjust to a life on the ground after having risen so far above it. It was like becoming a baby all over again, while at the same time remaining an adult. In fact, I actually saw somethings from the ground this time I somehow missed the first time, that have broadened my perspective about life.

"Made me realize how some things in Nature evolve beyond others sometimes, and that once anyone of us has grown, we can never allow ourselves to forget that those who haven't grown aren't too eager to be reminded of how much they still haven't changed. Especially by someone who used to be in a lowlier position than they were before that someone outgrew them. It's like a very unpleasant reminder of how limited, apathetic, and primitive they still are, and have always been. So you had to clip my wings, Almighty Mantis. I know it wasn't personal, but because Universal law mandated you perform the act for the purpose of providing me with the opportunity for being initiated into a higher self-awareness, and an expansion of consciousness.

"You've made it possible for me to evolve into someone who I never knew it was possible to become. After I grew my first set of wings, I thought I had finally achieved my highest level of greatness, and the acme of maturity, but I was sadly mistaken. Do you understand what I'm saying?"

"Why wouldn't I understand? Aren't you explaining to me how maturity is one third physical, and that your psychic, and spiritual maturation are far more important than the physical? That just because you had grown from a caterpillar into a butterfly physically, it didn't mean you had become a butterfly in every aspect.

"Isn't that what you're implying you beautiful tenacious caterpillar?"

"Yes that's precisely what I am saying. I realize now that my inner-self hadn't developed along with my outer self, and it took for you to bring about my inevitable fall from Heaven by clipping my wings. I am now self-aware, and self-realized enough to see that one cannot truly be in Heaven if they're not completely conscious of being in it. I was in Heaven before you clipped my wings, but I didn't know or appreciate my elevated position because I had forgotten what it was like when I was in Hell. I forgot what I evolved out of because my physical body involuntarily underwent a growth change beyond my conscious control, and placed me in Paradise unaccompanied by the awareness that my inner-self remained underdeveloped. So I unconsciously regenerated a self-created Hell I would someday become the denizen of, but I've noticed you still refer to me as the same beautiful caterpillar you always have. So what's up with that Mr. Almighty Mantis?"

"Why? Does that name bother you? Do you feel you deserve to be called something different? I mean, just because your opinion of yourself has changed doesn't mean mine, or anyone else's has to! Or does it?"

"Well, I guess that all depends upon who you're talking about, what the circumstances are, and what they desire to accomplish in every situation they find themselves in…

"What I mean is that I need to be more analytical, and self-aware around others so that I can perform differently. I've learned that if other people misperceive who I really am, I'm partially responsible. I've definitely learned the power of humility, and I don't have anything to prove to anyone besides myself, and it's impossible to please everyone all the time. So to answer your question I guess I've come to see how important it is to have a clear and concise concept of how other people feel about themselves before I show them my whole hand ever again.

"When my status changed from caterpillar to butterfly I was so overjoyed by the improvements that I lost sight of how little everyone else's reality changed. That when I changed, those who hadn't changed, had no need for being reminded by me just how much. So, now, thanks to you, I'm proud to confess that I got the message loud and clear. I haven't grown these beautiful wings back just to have them clipped all over again."

"Well Mr. Butterfly, it appears as though you have undergone some sort of inner transfiguration finally. You sound very convincing, and I hope you will be able from this day forward to actually be everything I hear you saying.

"I never intended to do any irreparable damage to you. I'm far more advanced than that, and it's my true desire to see you live a life of complete freedom, and inner tranquility from now on. So, is there anything else you came here to say today?"

"Well, only that I think it's about time I get back to the business of travelling, and go back to some of the places I've been before with my new insight. I want to go back and serve some of the other souls I've encountered in the past. The next time I take to the sky I'll reflect as I'm flying over all of the things that happened between the spider, bull frog, and chameleon in finer detail. So with that I say, Peace be unto you, Almighty Praying Mantis, until we meet again," and then flew away.

Fear of Flying

At times I'm a caterpillar with a perspective from the ground...
When things are too high for my perceptions, I bring them down...
I watch the wasps, the bees, and even the hawks...
And I envision the day when I'll be up there to talk...
I envy the flight, and honey of the bee, but not its sting...
I envy the flight of birds, and have it within myself to grow wings...
I envy the vision of the eagle, but I never despise...
At times I'm a caterpillar, desirous to loan you my eyes...
At other times I'm a butterfly with a perspective so very broad...
And whenever it's necessary, I can behave like a frog...
I can hop around on land, or hide myself in water so deep...
Irregardless of the form I assume, I'm never asleep...
Whenever I'm a frog, my constant concern is my lungs...
Whenever I'm flying high as a butterfly, I study tongues...
I envy that formless energy animating every form...
At times I'm a caterpillar who wishes his body was never born...
Sometimes I enjoy the low position, and sometimes the high...
It's the privilege of both positions that proves I'll never die...
I can be a rock, a rose, a buffalo, or even a conscious man...
I know deep within myself I'm everything with a consciousness that expands...
Every time I'm a caterpillar I'm at my best because I desire to be greater...
Anytime I'm a butterfly I become disgusted by all the haters...
Most of the time I realize it's best to just be an unnoticeable caterpillar...
Last time I was a butterfly I saw too many killers...!!!

Seventh Retrospection

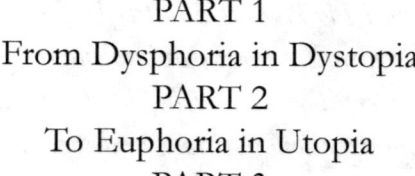

PART 1
From Dysphoria in Dystopia
PART 2
To Euphoria in Utopia
PART 3
Sempiternal Soliloquist

Butterfly – 2. A person interested principally in frivolous behavior (a social butterfly.)

Monologue – A long speech made by one person. 2. A dramatic soliloquy. 3. A literary composition in the form of soliloquy.

Sophism – The theory that the self is the only thing that can be known and verified. 2. The theory or view that the self is the only reality.

Soliloquy – A literary dramatic form of discourse in which a character talks to himself or reveals his thoughts in the form of a monologue without addressing the listener. 2. The act of speaking to oneself.

Dysphoria – Emotional state characterized by anxiety, depression, and restlessness.

Dystopia – An imaginary place, as a country of total misery and wretchedness.

Euphoria – A feeling of intense excitement and happiness.

Utopia – An imaginary place or state of things in which everything is perfect.

Sempiternal – Eternal and unchanging; everlasting.

*Within
Every Man
there exists a caterpillar,
who is being watched by the spider,
who waits for It to become ensnared
by a web of its spinning.
All because he forgets he was once
a tadpole in the Infinite waters of
Mother Space,
who nurtured him until he became
ready to be a creature capable of living
on the land.
Making it possible for him to function
as a chameleon who reflexively
adapts to, and blends in with
its environment.
Giving him the space and freedom
required for developing into the
mantic individual who follows the
impersonal laws of nature effortlessly.
His very istence becomes a prayer that never
ends because his consciousness is elevated
like the beautiful butterfly who proves
the resilience, and immortality
of the
Human Spirit…*

Now that he'd had the opportunity to converse with every individual who played a part in bringing him back down to Earth he was finally feeling complete.

His spiritual downfall on the doomsday his wings were clipped was a tragedy he never saw coming, but now he was glad it had occurred.

His fall gave him the chance to re-evaluate himself, and realize that being a butterfly was about more than the gratification of his insatiable desire for pleasure.

He reflected while in the air over his earliest days as a caterpillar, being limited, and preyed upon by the friendly neighborhood spider. He remembered the constant anxiety, restlessness, and oppressiveness he wrestled with, and feeling like the world is a miserable, wretched place, where pain and suffering are the only things any sentient beings ever have to look forward to.

Every day feeling desperate for an easier and more comfortable existence where he didn't have to struggle to provide his basic needs for survival.

Desperate for a pain-free life of untroubled ease, where everyone wanted for their neighbor what they wanted for themselves, and would even sacrifice their own self-interest to make such a high ideal an actual reality.

He used to observe the spider from his limited view, and wonder whether or not he felt the same way, or if it were even possible for him to since he was in a more privileged position than himself. He wondered how a creature with so much mobility, and so many other options could ever experience any type of dissatisfaction similar to his own.

Due to the caterpillar's unawareness of its inherent potential for becoming greater, he was envious of the spider, and would've been more than happy to switch positions with him at any time. Yet he was fearful of the spider's power to entangle him in one of its transparent webs it so strategically spun in every unsuspecting location of the neighborhood.

Then the thought entered his mind that maybe the spider, along with the bull frog, and chameleon, had seen something within him he hadn't even known was there until he actually became it. Was it possible that maybe they'd seen so many other before who lived a portion of their lives in a state of unconscious-consciousness. Many who eventually outgrew all of them just as he'd been destined to from the very beginning, and secretly despised them for it all along?

If this was true then it explained why they conspired against him while he'd been away, and waited for him to return so Mother Nature could show him her tough love to those who failed to appreciate their gifts. How one's gifts so easily become their curse by being irresponsible with, and unappreciative of them.

As the butterfly soliloquized in deep consternation as to why they didn't tell him what they knew was in him, his dystopian disposition began to seem more justifiable to him. He couldn't see any reason why he ought to feel any differently about the world than he had when he was still a wriggling worm confined to the Earth.

In retrospect, it was now clear to him that the three of them were envious, and cowardly from the beginning, and never liked the fact that he was predestined to become more highly evolved than they. That it had been their cruel intentions from the outset to destroy him for having it within himself to become everything they wanted to be, but never could.

Was it true they could never become like him, because it was not within Nature's Plan, or did they just have to wait their turn. Was there actually a time in his own past, forgotten history when he'd been a spider, bull frog, or a chameleon internally who would eventually develop the elevated self-consciousness of the impersonal Praying Mantis?

Perhaps each one of them was conscious of this natural law, and the reason why he had to forgive them for being the only individuals they had it within themselves to be at those particular stages of their personal growth and development.

It was in this very moment he began recounting the last hours he'd spent with the spider, and the mystic conversation they had. He remembered the profound statement the spider made during the intervals between his last breaths. When he said, "You mustn't feel sorry for me because what is happening to me right now, is happening to you also, and is a part of life."

What did the spider mean by that? Was the spider saying he was dying too with every breath he took? Or that there was a spider inside of him that was dying so that a new aspect of himself could come to life? Or was it just another one of the spider's sarcastic remarks made to irritate him, like the butterfly irritated him the day he winked his eye and flew away? Perhaps it was all three of them?

Then, upon further reflection, it dawned on the butterfly that the spider shared some of its wise foresight about cycles within cycles in this great mystery of life itself. The spider had been around for a very long time before its death, and saw not only him, but many other things come and go. Plus the spider only made the remark after the caterpillar lost its first set of wings, and confined to the Earth for the second time around.

Then he thought about the time he spent in the cocoon, and the many different painful phases he passed through to becoming a flying creature. How being in the cocoon must be synonymous to the place where the spider was headed once it breathed its last breath before the sudden Earthquake, and that there are no deaths, or endings for anything in existence. Just graduations and transformations.

How it must be true that all things like the caterpillar becoming a butterfly, become greater in time, and that the spider must've known from watching the caterpillar's transformation, that they were both intrinsically the same.

So the spider made sure to mention while passing on, "Don't cry, or have pity on me my old friend. You must not feel sorry for me because what is happening to me right now, is happening to you also."

Could he have been wrong all along about the spider wishing to make a meal of him while he was still a worm? Or was he just awaiting his own day of transformation into another one of the beautiful aerial creatures he'd been observing throughout its lifetime?

After all the spider did say during their last conversation that his brightest memory of him was the day he looked up and saw him sitting on the edge of the roof, flapping his new set of wings proudly, and arrogantly. How he shot him that vain glorious eye wink just before flying away. He told the butterfly who at that time had resumed his lower class, caterpillar status that it was the reason he was crawling on the ground again.

Had he completely misperceived the spider's intentions toward him from the very beginning? Had he himself been the sole creator of every tragedy he survived through prior to his reascension into the Heavens? Could he have somehow prevented those things from occurring by behaving differently towards some of the less fortunate individuals in the neighborhood before his preordained period of confinement?

Black Butterfly

Everything within, screaming for an outlet, is finally coming forth…
Everything that pushed me to become an addict, and shrouded in darkness, transformed into a torch…
Everything Buddha, Moses, Jesus, and Muhammad taught lies latent within humanity's collective consciousness…
Everything the human body is enslaved by, dulls the human spirit's responsiveness…
Everything I write is an explanation of Everything I've encountered on The Path…
Everything I've ever thought, said, or done is my Karmic Ledger of Divine pleasure, or wrath…
Everything I experience presently is just the sum total of Everything my thoughts created for me in the past…
Everything anyone has ever seen materialize is the product of living unmanifested Math…
Everything any human being does, has done, or ever shall do, has a hidden motive…
Everything no one has the desire, or courage to even look at, I try to expose, and quote it…
Everything that has lead me to hate, has lead me to love myself, and understand the world…
Everything that happens in life is like a wise old woman who must be cultured while she's still a little girl…
Everything that seems uncommon becomes common for anyone courageous enough to be honest and open…
Everything changing no longer causes me pain, because the Divine Scheme may be inconsistent with what I'm hopin'…

The Caterpillar & The Spider

Everything fear produces is scary to any coward who allows their inner-spirit to be broken…
Everything addiction held captive, recovery is pushing to the surface…
Everything I've done, and examination of my crimes, is transfiguring me into a candidate for service…
Everything that now brings me calm in life, are the very same things that once made me nervous…
Everything I used to perceive as the enemy, is now a friend-emy, because I re-cognize its purpose…
Everything, Everyone, does to Anyone, is meant to happen to them, or it wouldn't…
Everything that is Anything, to Some-thing, is meant to be exactly what it is to them, or it just couldn't…
Everything we think, or were thinking, has been thought of before, so how can we say things Shouldn't…
"Every-thing is All there is, appearing as any-thing, some-thing, and many things, so us things can see Every-thing."

—by the Cater-fly

It was becoming more depressing, while at the same time more clear to the butterfly, all of the reasons why there was no way he could've prevented himself from falling the first time.

He realized his ignorance of his inherent capability he'd been created with could've only been brought to his awareness through his own self-generated suffering. That the spider was only the physical reflection of the Elder consciousness within himself, performing the preordained task prescribed by the fixed laws of the Universe.

The law which determines that there can be no emotional, or soul growth for any individual without the extra effort stimulated by pain.

No one shall receive any spiritual benefits until they have proven by their steadfastness in the face of adversity, that they truly deserve them.

He was realizing the miserable, and wretched emotional state he'd been living in for so long was the result of his own distorted perceptions about life, himself, and reality in general. As he coasted over the countryside that held so many memories, and life lessons, he thought intensely about the bull frog's participation in bringing him down.

If the spider symbolized the Elder consciousness within, who spun the web of its own self-deception, and hypnosis, in order to later go back and receive the benefits of the foods which were caught in the web; then the bull frog must've held a similar significance as well, but what was it exactly?

He knew the bull frog too had undergone its own morphological transformation, which must've been irrefutable proof that its involvement in this Divine dramatic plot was also by the will of a Grand Architect, with a Grand design already inscribed upon the Infinite cycle of Eternal progression.

So now he just had to reflect over the stages of development the bull frog passed through on its way to becoming itself.

Retrospectively, the butterfly realized that if the spider was the forerunner who knew the end at the beginning, then the bull frog's purpose was to prompt him to critically analyze and examine his own origins.

So he travelled back into his own history while soaring through the air to a time when he, like the bull frog, must've been just a tiny egg amongst many, immersed in water for a certain length of time. An egg that eventually hatched and remained confined to a particular set of circumstances, and whose mobility remained limited until the time was ripe for it to become more suitable for advancement.

He saw that not only him, but every-thing must undergo stages of growth and maturity before reaching the prescribed point for them assigned by their Karmic Ledger.

The bull frog, like himself, was once a tadpole immersed in water, who eventually because a land rover; but the bull frog's evolution was not to go beyond that point. He was to remain a swimmer, and a land rover throughout his entire existence until…

However, from the water to the land is the journey of every living soul. Being able to recognize the benefits which accrue one's aquatic life is definitely something all should someday have the desire to understand. The depths have always been the place where life's greatest treasures lie hidden, and where few have ever developed the iron will necessary for plunging into, and going in search of the jewels they shall most certainly uncover.

It was this deep place within the butterfly failed to take notice of for the majority of its life, and the main reason he had to be struck down. He may not have been able to enter the watery depths physically like the bull frog, but he could most certainly travel there mentally.

Deep within the depths of his own soul in order to extract the hidden wisdom that had been there throughout Eternity, and potentially remain hidden even longer had he never been knocked out of the sky for a time.

When he was still just a groveling little land worm he experienced things which were an immense storehouse of valuable lessons, but he never noticed because he was too busy being depressed, and complaining unto himself over his limitations. He focused so much on them he became incapable of recognizing his inherent limitless potential.

Then when Nature finally elevated him to favorable heights with a new set of wings to soar the skies, and view the world from an entirely new and different perspective; he took it for granted, and forgot about everything he'd survived through before being reinstated.

His fall enabled him to come into contact with, and identify his Elder Spider Self. He probably would've never recognized the benefits of the sudden Earthquake that obscured the spider, yet paradoxically made it more translucent, and meaningful. The spider's physical presence in his life hindered him from seeing its spiritual significance within the evolution of his own consciousness.

When he was still a caterpillar the spider's presence kept him alert. He was the mortal adversary Nature strategically put in his life to help him become the conqueror he was predestined to become. The necessary opposing force who impassioned him to someday lift himself off of the ground for the sake of showing forth Life's wondrous, and beautiful transmigrations, and transfigurations.

Once he became a butterfly he failed to take notice of the arrogant, vindictive, and petty minded spirit such an involuntary transformation had given birth to. His purpose for becoming a butterfly wasn't for becoming addicted to enjoyment, or using his gift of flying for looking down upon the creatures who were unable to ascend to his level.

He had a divine obligation to begin viewing the spider as a special friend sent by the Universe in the guise of an enemy to teach him some valuable lessons, but he failed to do so, and was forced to suffer the inevitable consequences.

Upon inception of the new set of wings, his outlook on life renewed itself as well. He had graduated to the conscious awareness of the chameleon within himself, and learned to utilize his colors to blend into any environment. He was becoming adept at shining without actually shining. How to make a difference without appearing to be different. How to stand out while he stood in.

His entire life had been an endless series of transformations from the very beginning, but he spent the first half of it involuntarily transforming. He appreciated every growing pain he ever experienced in his past, and was no longer bitter about the things done to him by the friends he believed betrayed him. It wasn't they who were at fault, but only his distorted perceptions of what friendship truly is that was the problem. His own faulty perceptions wound up causing him to make decisions that were not in his best interest.

His own naivete about the nature of individuals who remain underachievers, while they watch others around them go on to achieve great things, misled him into believing that everyone from his old neighborhood was going to be delighted when he returned, but he'd been a fool.

The overpowering emotion of envy pushes those less-talented, or less-fortunate than ourselves to feel inferior, and wish to see those they deem to be superior to themselves either helpless, hurt, or dead.

The butterfly returned to his homeland with false hopes that the ones he left behind were going to be happy he went away, and became someone better than he used to be, and that they were going to be congratulatory, complimentary, and anxious to have him share with them the details of his great adventures.

He'd been dangerously inconsiderate, and unmindful of the fact that they remained the same limited individuals, who never left the same dreadful environment they'd all grown up in, and still lacking the belief in themselves it took to become more highly evolved beings. He forgot the true nature of the individuals he rose up, and flew away from, or that they plotted, and were waiting for the first opportunity that presented itself to remind him.

Was it ever even sensible to believe that those who are confined to a limited degree of progress could ever be happy about the elevation and limitlessness of their more highly advanced brothers and sisters?

Shouldn't the more advanced, and naturally gifted individuals expect to be envied by the weak, faithless underachievers who are unable to recognize their own inherent potential for genius?

The caterpillar had a more realistic conception of their environment, and the dangers within it than the butterfly. The butterfly forgot how good he had it until he was forced to live like a caterpillar all over again. Now that he had his wings back, he vowed he would never be so ignorant, and shortsighted again. He was ready to be responsible, and protective of his gift in order to prevent the self-induced suffering produced by his own self-deceptive ignorance.

The butterfly was finally happy, and felt a sense of security now, unlike anything he ever felt before. His new realistic outlook on life, and the other souls in it, made him certain he would be able to perform in every future situation like a wise, clairvoyant creature who would see the effects of his actions before performing them. Thus giving him the power to create the life for himself he knew was possible, after having had a taste of it already before the fall.

Now he was ready to fly while still crawling on the ground. He was ready to let himself be seen by everyone out in the open while he still hid his real self from view like the spider hides itself away for many years in attics and caves. He was ready to be plain and unassuming on land, while still hiding in the depths of the depths of the deepest water like the bull frog who never forgets it was once a tadpole. He was ready to show off his beautiful colors while blending in with his environment effortlessly like the humble chameleon.

Most of all he was willing to be emotionally resilient, ruthless, and impersonal towards himself and every person, place, or thing around him whenever the occasion required he be so, like the Almighty Praying Mantis. He had finally grown up, and learned how to fly.

The Wisdom Lying Somewhere Between the Butterpillar & the Caterfly

Everyone from the neighborhood who conspired to bring about his downfall had passed away, or were they somewhere in the Universe in an invisible cocoon, soon to emerge as some-thing superior to what they'd been?

The Summer was quickly coming to a close, and the time for our friend to make its pilgrimage to New Mexico for laying eggs and passing on, very near.

Due to deep contemplation, and self-reflection, our friendly neighborhood caterfly was now ready to live the remainder of its life in is-tence, as a butterpillar.

Its new purpose became to live a lot more unselfishly, and much more like the impersonal Praying Mantis.

The one who clipped his wings, and forced the butterfly to have to see things from the caterpillar's perspective all over again.

Who brought about its life changing self-realization, enabling it to obtain a clear, and concise understanding of how every individual involved in the plot to bring him down, were really living embodiments of his own developmental stages.

As a butterpillar, he took things back to the beginning, when the Spider had it within its power to take his life, but didn't.

Remembering its days as a caterpillar, and carrying around the constant fear and paranoia associated with the belief that the Spider intended to end its existence.

Being totally ignorant of the fact that its own negative, fear-based thinking, was actually creating the reality it feared so much.

Choosing to live life in the future as a butterpillar meant living life humbly, and with the self-awareness that true greatness lies within one's ability to remain cognizant of the fact that no matter how high we ascend, descension begins when we become complacent, and adopt the false notion we can ascend no higher.

Rising above his own selfish ignorance had been the key to freedom even when he was a caterpillar, but by constantly comparing itself to everything else in Nature that appeared to be more gifted, and highly favored than itself, it was stunting its own growth, and development.

By asking itself; "What purpose could I have given to my life if I would've remained a caterpillar forever?", became the most self-liberating question it ever asked itself.

By reflecting upon the idea of remaining a caterpillar forever, and how it could've given purpose to its life in such a lowly position, it figured out that one's inability to have empathy for others, and how much worse life could've been, instantly gave the butterpillar's life new meaning.

To be a selfless co-worker with nature, by being able to accept the positions we find ourselves in without becoming bitter, resentful, and angry; until through our own efforts at maintaining a resilient, and tenacious attitude, we eventually reap the benefits for being so. We're able to enjoy the fortune provided by ease and comfort from elevating ourselves to a relative level of self-mastery.

By returning to its own humble origins, and thinking about the pilgrimage it was soon to embark upon to New Mexico in order to lay eggs. Then passing on and becoming a disembodied consciousness shortly afterwards, whose elements would return to the Earth from which it came to eventually be reused by the Universe in whatever capacity prescribed by the Grand Designer.

Such reflection helped the butterpillar to free itself from the psychological bondage it had been held captive by for most of its life.

Then it dawned on the caterfly that it had one last selfless act to perform before leaving its old stomping grounds once and for all.

Being a butterpillar meant being self-aware enough to realize the times it would need to lower its wings, and take on the perspective of the caterfly in order to practice the humility required for understanding its obligatory responsibility for selfless service.

This meant going to check on the current status of the eggs left behind by his friendly late Spider, and figuring out what he could do to insure they made it into the world safely.

Remembering them being located in the old tool shed right next to the old house the Spider once lived, and died in, he made his way there. As he approached he saw the Praying Mantis angling on a corner of the shed, looking into it as if ready to attack and pounce on whatever was under observation.

This time however, before allowing any presumptions, or unsubstantiated fear to take control, the butterpillar made a conscious decision in the heat of its passion to become the caterfly, and remain open to the possibility for a new experience unlike any other from the past.

Quickly recalling that he'd already experienced the worst life could throw at him, and that his physical existence was coming to an end, there was absolutely no reason at all to be fearful, or apprehensive in the slightest bit.

Upon reaching the praying mantis, after brief, but careful deliberation, he heard, "Oh, look who finally decided to show up!"

"And just what is that supposed to mean?" said the caterfly.

"Well I've been waiting for you to get here so that you could see what's going on in here."

"Wait a minute. You mean you've known all along about the spider's eggs?"

"Of course I have. Or have you forgotten the spider and I knew each other very well, and long before you were even here Mr. Caterfly! You should know by now that there's not much going on around here that I don't know about! I'm here to make sure they get looked after just in case you've yet to become the butterpillar/caterfly, and decided not to show up.

"Obviously though, you've managed to wisen up, and you're not the same beautiful caterpillar with wings you used to be!"

"Well, let's just say I've learned enough to know that you did me a favor when you clipped my wings, and because of it there's still a whole lot more I still need to learn-."

"Glad to hear that you beautiful butterpillar! I hate to be rude, but it's very important you inch your way over here and take a look…"

"Oh myyyyyah," said the butterpillar. "I see the eggs have finally hatched. They're crawling all over the place. So I guess we've done our duty, and that they'll figure things out from here? Right? Whaddayu think my friend?"

"Well, beside the fact that we should probably introduce ourselves, and let them know we knew their birth-giver, I suppose you're correct.

"That way the future offspring of your species will have the opportunity to perhaps receive even more mercy than you received from our dearly departed old friend. Wouldn't you agree?"

"I can see how that makes perfect sense Mr. Almighty Praying Mantis! I concur…"

So they did exactly that, and afterwards the Mantic-Mantis said, "Listen you beautiful butterpillar! I really could do without the sarcastic undertone, and would appreciate it if you no longer refer to me as the Almighty. I hold no superiority over you, and I'm proud to say that it's been quite a pleasure to have made your acquaintance. I truly believe you've earned the title of "Beautiful Butterfly" now, and I'm pretty sure your journey henceforward shall be a very edifying, and philanthropic one."

"Thank you very much Sir!" the butterfly said, as he turned to catch another glimpse of the newborn spiders, but when he spun back around the Praying Mantis was gone.

He combed the area with his eyes, but didn't see him anywhere. So he chuckled, and felt a sense of overwhelming joy, and inner peace overcome him.

A feeling of relief, and accomplishment, confident that the resistance he'd always felt the haunting presence of no longer existed.

Freedom now meant, that as a more highly evolved being there comes the responsibility of caring for all living things, and doing what is within our power to assist in their natural progression right along with our own.

Higher enlightenment must be accompanied by a heightened awareness that selfishness is the highest form of ignorance, and that when we learn to live more for others, and less for ourselves, we become empathetic thinkers, with purer hearts, and desiring the indiscriminate unity of all people, and every living thing.

Flying high is never about seeking the inner peace, and tranquility we falsely believe can be obtained by amassing the material things that bring fame, power, and sensual pleasure.

All of the things King Solomon attests to having amassed in the Book of Ecclesiastes, and he described as, "vanity of all vanities", or "a chasing after the wind".

The butterfly's ideas about itself had changed, and it now believed that knowing when to be the caterfly, or the butterpillar ideally transfigured him into the creature Nature intended for him to be.

So, he turned and said farewell to the newborn spiders, and hit the skies at the approach of the Autumnal Equinox.

This would be the last time he ever saw his old stomping grounds, or better yet training grounds. It felt right though, because he'd achieved redemption, and complete vindication.

He was no longer trapped in the web spun by his own self-deceptive misery, generated by selfish ignorance, but free to be the butterfly whose altruism, and aestheticism captivates the hearts of every onlooker who shall ever behold it…

The Caterpillar & The Spider

Epilogue

As he flew away, I thought about the instructive words of Confucius who said: "The higher man practices before he preaches, and then preaches according to his practice."

I thought over this because throughout the years, so many people, myself included, have appeared to be hypocrites due to not practicing many of the things we so passionately advocate. When the fact is we've become experts at conceptualizing, and verbalizing so well many of the things that would make us into living saints if we practiced them. Though the reality is that the majority of us rarely put into practice more than one-third of what we know, and learn.

Because it's so much easier to imagine, and discuss the highest ideals, than it is to actually BE them, most of us fall short of embodying these ideals. Since it takes far less courage, willpower, and self-discipline to take the low road instead of the high when we're still young, and inexperienced.

I thought about how much more important it is to be beautiful, and majestic within, by possessing a self-awareness that makes it possible for us to put into practice those behaviors, and attitudes, which exemplify those who possess the hearts of empathetic thinkers.

Appearing beautiful on the outside, with very little, to absolutely no inner awareness about how to treat others, or respond to our environments doesn't take us very far in life. Gaining mastery over ourselves, and our environments is a process, and without the help of Elder, more wise, and experienced individuals in our lives, the desire to achieve such mastery may not take root within many until they've endured and overcome tremendous amounts of suffering, and passed through a series of painstaking transformations.

With this I bid you farewell, and hope this tale of "The Caterpillar and the Spider" becomes the spark that ignites the fire within required for becoming the empathetic thinking creatures who understand that being elevated means being, and spreading peace and harmony, in whatever circumstances we find ourselves in, or whomever we might be surrounded by.

Thank You

CHRYSALIS

Arise each mornin' a caterpillar, lie down for rest a butterfly...
Arise each mornin' a caterpillar, lie down for rest a butterfly...
Arise each mornin' a caterpillar, lie down for rest a butterfly...
Jump to give this thing called Life another try!
But isn't to try to fail? Isn't it just do or die...?
Is there any such thing as failure, since it's all part of an ongoing process...?
Then let us not judge ourselves based upon what we've yet to achieve, and remain focused upon our progress...
Until pain-ful becomes pain-less, there's still much more work to be done...
It still burns my eyes to look directly into the Sun...!
Why even get up and fight again, when it's so much easier to just lie down and die...?
Why not just limit myself to caterpillar nightmares, and only having dreams of touching the Sky...?
I've been living this nightmare for years, suspended in a cocoon, as I toss & turn to understand why...
Maybe I'm really a butterfly having nightmares of living the caterpillar's dream, with a nature to Reawaken and Fly...?

—One of the Little Ones About the Author

The Caterpillar & The Spider

ABOUT THE AUTHOR

After a life filled with a series of successive deaths and rebirths, and the excruciating pains associated with the psycho-existential dilemma caused by inherited misconceptions about what Life really is – the author came to the realization that chasing after an idealistic state of emotional contentment is actually inconsistent with reality. Pain can be a propellant.

Life is painful. However, the ability to alchemize one's pain, and convert pain's energy into a creative impetus, rather than a destructive hammer, is something I had to learn the hard way.

I had to learn that Life itself is not out to help or hurt me, and it is my responsibility to feel the pain, and return back to a state somewhere between euphoria and dysphoria. Just because Life can never be utopian doesn't mean it should be perceived as dystopian either.

Just because Life doesn't seem to be providing me with some of my wants and needs is no proof of anything. The key is to never take Life's ups and downs personally and keep moving forward despite its hardships. Never be afraid to fly, or to fall.

Thank you.

www.ingramcontent.com/pod-product-compliance
Lightning Source LLC
Chambersburg PA
CBHW071915070526
44583CB00016B/1995